GLORY
FROM
DEFEAT

GLORY FROM DEFEAT

OUR SECOND DUNKIRK

by

June Goodfield

June Goodfield

MENIN HOUSE

Menin House an imprint of
Tommies Guides Military Booksellers & Publishers
PO Box 3229
Eastbourne
East Sussex
BN21 9RZ

First published in Great Britain by
Tommies Guides, 2019

978-1-9998900-7-0

Cover design and typesetting by Ryan Gearing

Printed and bound in Great Britain

CONTENTS

DEDICATION

To the memory of those who did not return

Tread lightly with care
On the fresh earth of Europe
For this soil was once
The still eyes of young men.
The War Memorial, by Donald John MacDonald.

LIST OF ILLUSTRATIONS

FOREWORD

Alastair Dorward

FORMED in 1908, in a reshuffle of the then Territorial Army, as a formation comprising the kilted Highland infantry regiments, the 51st Highland Division, went on to give distinguished and noble service over nearly 60 years, including two world wars. During those years it earned a much-respected reputation for its valour and fighting capability and has a rightful place in Scottish military history as its foremost fighting force.

Disbanded in 1967 following a review of the armed forces, the fine traditions and fighting spirit of 51st Highland Division are today proudly maintained by the Highland battalions of the Royal Regiment of Scotland.

Of course, and regrettably, such a fine record of service cannot be achieved without considerable sacrifice and certainly one of the more profound instances was the defensive perimeter operation by the Division in

1940 around St Valery and the town of Veules les Roses – an action which lies at the heart of June Goodfield's book.

Standing in the sunshine at the top of the cliffs above Veules les Roses, after the dedication of the path named "Sentier Derek Lang" on a sunny afternoon in 2015, it would have been hard to imagine the events that took place just a few yards away 75 years before. It was here that many of the men of the 51st Highland Division were marched to captivity while others risked the descent of the cliffs on rifle slings, some crashing to their deaths. The more fortunate survived and were rescued by the gallant flotillas from Newhaven and Eastbourne.

June Goodfield has brought to life those last days of the 51st Highland Division in June 1940, in a wonderful account combining both past and present and the rich link between Alfriston and Veules les Roses.

She reminds us of the high price paid by the 51st Highland Division and the families of those who served. This is reflected on memorials in towns and villages throughout the Highlands. It is particularly poignant that they are also remembered where they fought protecting France. They are remembered in the Commonwealth War Graves Cemeteries, but also in local cemeteries and memorials erected by the people of Veules les Roses and St.Valery – and most touchingly by the children that took part in the recent ceremonies described in this book.

FOREWORD

The 51st Highland Division and Ross Bequest Trust are delighted to have been able to support this account which contributes to our understanding of the history of the Division. Seldom can a twinning have been so passionately developed and to such great effect.

Alastair Dorward,
Chairman 51st Highland Division
& Ross Bequest Trust

FOREWORD

Jean-Claude Claire

OUR two countries share a long history, which has left numerous traces: from William the Conqueror at Hastings in 1066; via the Treaty of London in 1358, which required that several provinces in South West France were yielded to England; the trial and martyrdom of Joan of Arc at Rouen on the 30th of May 1431; the peasants of the Pays de Caux who, in 1434, rose up against the English occupation and their harsh taxation.

More recently, the assassination of the Archduke of Austria, on June 28th 1914, led Europe into a world war and our two countries united their forces. Certain names and events will remain engraved forever in our memories: for example, the Allied offensive on the Somme; the terrible slaughter of Verdun; the USA entering the war against the German invader on 2nd April 1917.

The armistice signed at Rethondes on 11th November 1918 conceded victory to the Allies but at a terrible cost:

France lost 1,300,000 dead, Great Britain, 950,000. In 1933, Hitler came to power and on the 3rd September 1939, France and England declared war against Germany. Once again our two countries joined forces. Germany invaded Holland, Belgium and France and the battles were merciless. Nine days after Dunkirk, Saint Valery en Caux and Veules les Roses were surrounded by the German troops. Our soldiers, mostly from the 51st Highland Division, resisted as long as they could and showed immense heroism when trying to avoid being taken prisoner. Their sole aim was to reach England to continue the combat.

From Newhaven and Eastbourne boats of all shapes and sizes set sail in order to attempt to evacuate the Allied soldiers, but only 3,200 were saved. France will always be grateful to those who risked their lives for others.

In 2013, we decided that our two villages would be twinned. From that moment, a profound friendship on the British and the French sides was established. And now we meet twice a year with great joy continually trying to find what will give most pleasure to the others.

Come what may, it will always take a mere four hours to cross the Channel, and the bond uniting Alfriston to Veules les Roses is henceforth indissoluble.

Jean-Claude Claire
Maire de Veules les Roses
Chevalier, Order Légion d'Honneur

PREFACE

"I am proud to tell you that of all the
many fine Divisions
that served under me in the late war,
none was finer than the
Highland Division – none."

Field Marshal Sir Bernard Montgomery

THE story of Dunkirk – often referred to as the Miracle of Dunkirk – has been praised and commemorated in a multitude of ways – services of thanksgiving, music and many films. The British Expeditionary Force (BEF) – sent to aid the defence of France in September 1939, after the Germans invasion of Poland – fought alongside the French First, Seventh and Ninth Armies as well as the Belgian Army.

Eight months later, on 10th May 1940, Germany invaded, first the Netherlands, then Belgium and on 28th May, the Belgian Army surrendered. Yet nine days earlier the British commander, Lord Gort, learning that there were no French troops between the Germans and Channel, and that the Panzers were speeding towards to sea, immediately began planning a withdrawal to the nearest location with good port facilities and a long sandy beach. Here, at Dunkirk, the BEF was trapped.

By 4th June 1940, 338,226 British soldiers had been evacuated by 850 boats, and for generations, most people believed that they were the last on French soil.

They were not. Some 20,000 soldiers, mostly from the 51st Highland Division, remained in France and not until nine days after Dunkirk was there any chance of rescuing them. Yet the attempted evacuation would take place in Normandy – many miles to the west of Dunkirk ... and there was no miracle.

In September 1944, a whole three months after D-Day, the town of Veules les Roses, was the last coastal community in Normandy to be freed.

This book – a true story – is being written during the summer of 2018 in a small East Sussex village. In 2012 the communities of Alfriston and Veules les Roses, some fifteen kilometres to the west of Dieppe – established a formal Twinning relationship. This would prove hugely successful and many close friendships developed as adults and children exchanged visits. During our very first one to Veules we were taken to a special section of the cemetery – the last resting place of a number of Scottish soldiers. Many graves are marked simply – 'Unknown Soldier'.

Researching this history over the next few months, the author gradually unravelled events which were still not widely known – even in Scotland.

As Chairman of the Alfriston & Cuckmere Valley Twinning Association (ACVTA), the author discussed this history at length with M.le Maire, Jean Claude Claire, and his colleagues in the Marie at Veules. She then wrote to Lt Col Peter M Little, OBE, Commanding Officer of the Regiment into which the Division had been assimilated. She said that in September 2014, the two communities were planning to celebrate the seventieth anniversary of the town's liberation and might it be possible for a Regimental Highland Piper to be present. The moment he received this letter, Peter Little rang June. He expressed his delight that the story was at last being widely recognised and he would send a contingent of fifty soldiers to join the celebrations. None of us will ever forget the two days we spent with representatives from the Highland Regiment – in remembrance, celebration and at the end of the day, mutual enjoyment.

One year later, in June 2015, in an event lasting three days, attended by over four thousand people, we commemorated together the final battle, the surrender and the attempted evacuation undertaken by many courageous people.

Chapter 1

BATTLE

IN 1939 war was threating the whole of Europe, so much so that in April the British Minister of War, Hore-Belisha, declared that the Territorial Army must double its numbers. The Highland Division responded immediately and almost overnight the famous Highland regiments of Scotland – Camerons, Seaforth, Gordons, Argyll and the Black Watch – doubled in numbers in a speed of enlistment unmatched anywhere else in Britain.[1]

Shortly before his 25th birthday, on October 7th 1938, Derek Lang was made an acting, unpaid Captain in the Queen's Own Cameron Highlanders. On 30th November, Neville Chamberlain returned from his meeting with Hitler and on arrival at Heston airport, famously declared that it was to be *'peace in our time'*. But as Lang later wrote *"only the most naive of us believed it"*.

---

1   Eric Linklater – Foreword to Derek Lang's *Return to St Valery*

When six months later, Hore-Belisha's enlistment order came Lang had to recruit men across a vast area – from Morayshire in the east to the Outer Hebrides in the west – where sheep greatly outnumbered people. His officers were either ex-regulars, or farmers, or local professional men,

Derek Lang as young captain.

or sons of lairds working in the south and he was the only professional military link between Companies living many miles apart. So when ordered to double his strength from a *'rather uncertain'* five hundred men to twelve hundred, Lang confessed to understandable misgivings, for over and above the huge area he had to cover, there were many other difficulties. In one 4th Cameron Company, there were thirty-five MacDonalds and ten of them were called John; the weaponry throughout was just outmoded rifles and old Lewis guns. Though sadly lacking in military training the intense patriotism of the Highlanders soon reassured Lang, as did the cheering fact was that the finest bagpipe players in the world came from South Uist!

If pipers proved one consideration, kilts were another – a very serious matter indeed that pre-occupied the highest level of command. Should Highlanders be allowed into battle wearing kilts? The issue was attacked from three angles – security, difficulty of supply in war, inadequacy in case of gas attack. Never – ever – wearing any garments in the way of pants under the kilt, was a long standing tradition in all Highland regiments. So whatever the danger, eight yards of very thick tartan would surely give adequate protection. The authorities decided otherwise: anti-gas pants were issued and kilts forbidden – an order that was deeply resented and sometimes ignored.

By late August, 1939, general mobilisation was well on the way and the Highland Division was the first Territorial Division to join the newly formed British Expeditionary Force (BEF). By 1st September, all battalions and supporting arms and services of the 51st Highland Division were duly embodied and Major General Victor Fortune, who had fought with distinction with the Black Watch in the First World War, was in command. On the 16th September, they left Scotland and travelled by troop trains to Aldershot for final equipping and completion of training, preparatory to joining the BEF in France. On the political front, a solemn, public declaration of unity was issued by the supreme War Council of Britain and France.

British divisions were attached for periods of fifteen days to the French army stationed in front of the Maginot Line – which was allegedly impregnable. But in the early hours of 10th May, a major onslaught of Germans was unleashed on the Low Countries way to the north. Paratroopers landed in Holland; Panzers poured across the Belgium and Luxembourg frontiers. Holland surrendered within five days and on 15th May the French Premier telephoned Churchill and told him: *"We are defeated: we have lost the battle."*

Yet, Churchill was desperate to keep the grand Alliance in place and ensure that whatever the cost France went on fighting. So now the Highland Division was effectively placed under the command of the French.

On 20th May the Division was taken out of the Maginot Line and moved to the west. But the Germans soon broke through the French line, so separating the Division from the rest of the B.E.F. After a period of rest, when the next task for the Division was unclear, a move of 300 miles by road and rail, brought them to a position overlooking the river Bresle near Abbeville, just 80 miles east of Veules de Roses. So as the B.E.F. retired towards Dunkirk, the Division was left fighting with the French Army as part of the French IX Corps, striving to hold a line north west of Abbeville to the coast.

The reasons for the decisions made and who made them is still a question of debate. The title of Saul David's book *Churchill's Sacrifice of the Highland Division – France 1940*, sums up one prevalent view. In the first chapter he wrote:

"Arrive in the fashionable Norman coastal town of St Valery-en-Caux today, and you are hard pressed to

> *imagine the hell it was for thousands of trapped British*
> *soldiers of the 51st (Highland) Division on a June night*
> *in 1940, sacrificed by their government as a symbol*
> *of Allied unity in the war against Germany."*

The speed of the German advance, Blitzkrieg as it became known, was too fast for the Allies to react in a timely way or be fully aware of what was happening.

An article by Adam Sherwin – 7th July 2018 – says,

> *"...recently declassified files from the National*
> *Archives reveal that Churchill ordered the 51st to*
> *fight on in the days after the evacuation [of Dunkirk]*
> *despite a lack of rations, ammunition and transport.*
> *A commitment that the British Expeditionary Force*
> *(BEF) must move three brigades to reinforce struggling*
> *French divisions had to be honoured, lest the French*
> *capitulate, the war leader asserted."*

However, the introductory chapters in *St Valery: The Impossible Odds* by Bill Innes, written with the intention that some of the legends should be reassessed, clarify in great detail the chaotic sequence of events leading up to the fateful surrender on 12th June 1940.

So by 2nd June, while 70 miles away the bulk of the BEF and 30,000 French troops were being evacuated from Dunkirk, the bulk of the Highland Division were holding a

20-mile front. On 5th June Germans launched their main assault across the Somme and the whole Division was slowly forced backwards. By 8th June, with the situation becoming desperate, the War Cabinet wanted them to fall back towards Rouen so that they could be taken off from the port of Le Havre.

As Eric Linklater described:

> *"The German stream was driving the Division back along its whole front... The front was too long, its defenders too few. It was a physical numerical impossibility to hold so long line with only one division, and nowhere was it abandoned without fighting."*

The Highlanders' bravery throughout was acknowledged by Charles de Gaulle, then commander of the French armoured division. The future President said fighting alongside the 51st inspired his decision to keep fighting on the side of the Allies.

Chapter 2

SURRENDER

BY 2 June, while the bulk of the BEF and 30,000 French troops were being evacuated from Dunkirk, the Highland Division was still holding a twenty-mile front some seventy miles to the west.

On 7th June, General Fortune spoke to his brigadiers and senior officers:

> *"Gentlemen, I know you would not wish us to desert our French comrades. We could be back in Le Havre in two bounds. But they have no transport. We shall fight our way back with them, step-by-step".*

So during the next nine days the Highlanders fought unceasingly between the Somme and St Valery in Normandy. However, it would be the Seaforth and Camerons who, after a bitter surrender, would be trapped on dangerous cliffs above sloping sandy shores, and forced to endure the dangers of an attempted evacuation.

On 9th June the Luftwaffe bombed Le Havre and destroyed the Division's stores, leaving them critically short of both food and ammunition. General Fortune ordered Brigadier Stanley-Clarke, commanding 154 Brigade, to muster a force for the defence of Le Havre. This was formed in the village of Arques-la-Bataille and named 'Ark Force' after that village. Its task was to form a defensive position about 20 miles east of Le Havre, on the line Fécamp-Bolbec, through which the French corps and the 51st Highland Division would withdraw. They escaped Rommel's closing net with just minutes to spare and over the two nights of 11/12 and 12/13 June some 4000 men of 'Ark Force' were evacuated from Le Havre and taken to Cherbourg. Yet by the 10th June Rommel's 5th Panzer Division, having cut the road to Le Havre, had reached the Channel coast. Though an alternative move to Dieppe – just a day's journey for the Corps – was possible, records indicate that General Fortune had been led to believe – quite erroneously – that the approaches to the port had been mined and the harbour installations so damaged that Dieppe was utterly unsuitable for embarkation.

Thus the only place that offered any chance for evacuation was the small coastal town of St Valery-en-Caux even though, as a tidal harbour set in a small niche between towering cliffs, it would normally have been deemed unsuitable.

Beach at Veules looking towards St Valery

Yet by the early hours of 11 June a variety of circumstances and constraints had forced General Fortune to accept this town as the only option for embarkation. So he made plans to secure a bridgehead and set a perimeter around St Valery. Yet at a time when only quick and firm action could save the 51st Division, he was also constrained by a British Government equally preoccupied with the political repercussions. The Highlanders were tacitly under French command and in theory at least, could not leave French soil without French permission.

So while the German tanks were a mere six miles away, the bulk of the Highland Division began to fall back into a box perimeter around St Valery – following the line of the River Bethune. In front were the 4th Seaforths, 5th Gordons, and the 1st Black Watch from Veules-les-Rose to Fontaine-le-

29

Dieu. However, advancing from the west Rommel, who had already cut off the Division's retreat, launched a large-scale armoured assault with almost 100 tanks that broke through the defensive perimeter and drove the Division further back.

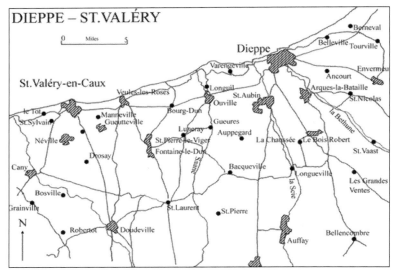

Map of Dieppe – St. Valery

Finally, General Fortune issued an Order of The Day: the Royal Navy would make an effort to take them off.

> *"The Navy will probably make an effort to take us off by boat, perhaps to-night, perhaps in two nights. I wish all ranks to realise that this can only be achieved by the full co-operation of everyone. Men may have to walk five or six miles. The utmost discipline must prevail.*

"Men will board the boats with equipment and carrying arms. Vehicles will be rendered useless without giving away what is being done. Carriers should be retained as the final rear-guard. Routes back to the nearest highway should be reconnoitred and officers detailed as guides. Finally, if the enemy should attack before the whole force is evacuated, all ranks must realise that it is up to them to defeat them. He may attack with tanks, and we have quite a number of anti-tank guns behind. If the infantry can stop the enemy's infantry that is all that is required, while anti-tank guns and rifles inflict casualties on armoured fighting vehicles."

So, while the men of the 51st Division were struggling into St Valery, an armada assembled by Admiral James was doing its best to make the proposed overnight rendezvous on June 11th –12th. Yet when at 17:00 on the 11th, Captain Warren in HMS Codrington, received a signal from Captain Tower in Le Havre, giving the go-ahead for the evacuation, all James's ships were still at sea- seven miles north-west of St Valery. Most did not even receive Tower's signal, for though the civilian rescue force consisted of 67 ships merchant ships and 140 smaller boats, only a mere 16 could receive radio messages. This severe handicap might not have been disruptive on a clear day, but the weather was anything but clear. Thick patches of fog drifted across the sea making contact by light signals impossible. So the boats drifted apart and soon lost touch.

St Valery was captured by the 7th Panzer Division: the French surrendered at 08:00 on the morning of 12th June and two hours later, General Fortune, having run out of all possible options, reluctantly also surrendered. He was taken prisoner along with four thousand French and eight thousand men from the Highland Division.

To Rommel's delight, his captives included the headquarters staff and their commander. As Desmond Young wrote in his book, '*Rommel*':

"Rommel never forgot Gen. Fortune and often spoke of him to his wife and son, Manfred, with sympathy as the gallant leader of a good Division who had had bad luck."

General Fortune (centre) with General Rommel (left) after surrender at St Valery

But some soldiers of the Highland Division were determined not to surrender and this led to 'Operation Cycle'.

Chapter 3

RESCUE

'OPERATION Cycle' took place from the 7th to 13th June 1940 when fishermen and boatmen from Rye, Hastings, Eastbourne, Newhaven and Brighton – all towns directly across the Channel – attempted an evacuation from Veules les Roses. The men of Eastbourne were the first to volunteer and their personal accounts are vivid.

In a letter dated 25th March 1990, written to a producer on Southern Television, Jean Allchorn said that her grandfather, her uncles and her future father in law, were amongst them. Ernie (Glaxo) Sayers, from the Fishermen's Institute in Eastbourne, crossed the Channel in a small open boat and would make a dramatic escape from the German attacks. He wrote:

> *"On June 10th all boats capable of crossing the Channel were ordered to report at a south coast*

port [Newhaven] and our small boat, with myself as skipper, and F. Allchorn as engineer, and Mr Prodger also skipper, arrived and found that several friends had already gone across.

"I well remember how agreeably surprised I was to see them arrive at Newhaven more than an hour before they were expected. This was due in no small measure to the efficiency of Police Sargeant Arnold who was responsible for informing the Eastbourne fishermen and getting them taken to the fishing station. He hustled them out of their beds in the middle of the night and they turned out as if for a lifeboat call. Those living in outlying parts of the town were collected by Mrs MacAlein and driven to the station in her car, where other willing helpers were assisting launching the boats. We signed on, and then had orders to stand by which we did all day and night. We then had orders to get rations for four days, got then aboard and were dished out with helmets and bandages, and finally we were taken in tow by a tug."

The 'Haven Blue' Flotilla – raised at Newhaven under the command of Lieutenant Dyer, consisted of nine motor yachts and three fishing boats in the tow of a coastal collier. They arrived at St Valery at 2pm on 11 June, but found no other craft in sight. The flotilla then sailed north for two hours, but still seeing nothing, presumed that all ships had been withdrawn. So they returned to Newhaven- and other boats did the same.

Nevertheless, despite the adverse weather conditions, poor communications and the lack of cooperation shown by some civilian sailors, many crews were determined to see the operation through and set out across the Channel again. When they finally arrived of St Valery during the hours of darkness... the whole town was burning fiercely and the beach was being pounded by intense machine-gun and artillery fire.

So shortly after 1.00 am, all boats that could be contacted, were directed to the quieter beach at Veules les Roses, four miles to the east.

The first ship of any size to reach Veules was the Goldfinch, commanded by Lt Thompson. By 2:30, three of his officers and 21 ratings, had manned their lifeboats and were picking up soldiers off the beach. Thompson's report shows his admiration for those he rescued:

> *"It was a revelation to see men who had been fighting today without proper food or rest, helping to pull the boat out to the ship, most of them were exhausted when they came aboard. Many were wounded."*

Although there was intermittent German fire during the early morning, rain and hazy weather reduced its effectiveness and nothing was hit. But at 8:30 am a heavy artillery bombardment from both the east and the west fell upon the boats and beach.

Another volunteer rescuer said,

> *"It was simply murder. There was a heavy fog, the sea was rough and the Germans were ready for us. It was like sending toys out to fight tanks. Flashes of gunfire from coastal batteries pierced the fog... Although it was a rescue expedition, we were determined to make it an offensive operation if we had a chance. In each craft there was a Lewis gun, its base hastily screwed to the deck. We had a rapid course of instruction – lasting just a few minutes in some cases.*
>
> *Our landings were attempted in the face of constant heavy and accurate shell fire from the cliff tops. After spending two days and nights in small boats the first flotilla returned to Newhaven where the tired crews were immediately relieved by naval personnel."*

Derek Lang also gave a vivid account the experience that ultimately led to his capture – one shared by many soldiers.

> *"On fifth day of the retreat we received the alarming message that there had been a complete breakthrough to the south-west and the Germans were already in Rouen. At the same time we had the first firm orders since we started. We were to make for Le Havre as*

fast as we could where the Royal Navy was waiting to ferry us back to England ...

... We had only done about 20 miles when we learnt that the road to Le Havre was cut and we were to make our way to the little fishing village of Saint Valery en Caux. It is a name which will be forever remembered in the annals of the 51st Highland Division. ... The next day we took up a defensive position round St Valery and at midnight moved in perfect order down from our positions to the little town.

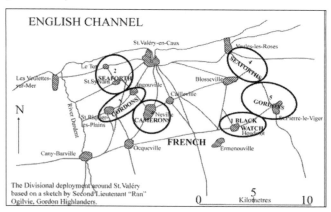

Map of disposition of Highland Divisions around St Valery

... As we filed down from the hills above the town we saw that it was ablaze ... The only solution seemed to be to make for the beach and to try to reach the ships which were to take us off. It was a vain dream. ... The Germans now commanded the beach from the heights on the west ... with the whole front ablaze we

were silhouetted against furiously burning fires and completely trapped.

When dawn finally broke hope rose again when two ships were spotted lying close in shore three to four miles down the coast at Veules les Roses. I found our acting Brigadier and suggested to him that I should try to reach one of these ships. If they had a wireless set working ... I would be able to get in touch with the Royal Navy and at least discover if there was any prospect of our being taken off. Ian agreed ... so I set off taking one of our Sgt Majors with me.

We had to keep close into the rocks to avoid attracting machine-gun fire from the cliff tops ... we came across the bodies of many of our soldiers and Frenchmen who had been caught in the crossfire of the guns. Some lay at the water's edge, washed by the tide. Others were poised in standing or crouching positions against the rocks where they had been shot ... their bodies rigid in death. Evidently some of the troops had tried to descend the 300ft high cliffs on ropes. Few could have succeeded judging by the smashed bodies lying on the beach while 150ft above we could see the frayed ends of their broken ropes. Most appalling of all were the wounded. They were everywhere...

"With the hard going and the heat, we discarded most of our clothing and were completely exhausted when, after two hours, we finally reached Veules. The

Rough seas at Veules today

bigger of the two ships was French and was lying some way out from the shore; the other, little more than a fishing boat, bravely flew the red ensign ... the decks of both ships were already covered with men, both French and British.

While were taking in the scene ... the big guns on the cliffs near St Valery opened up on the Frenchmen ... we had a ringside seat at this macabre play, watching in horror as they systematically destroyed the crowded ship.

The Germans turned their attention to the British ship and I decided to make a dash for her in the hope I could find a wireless set before it was destroyed. As I clambered aboard the first person I met was

Colin Hunter, the Intelligence Officer from my own Battalion ... I quickly learnt that there was no wireless and that the boat was so hopelessly overcrowded that the Captain feared she would not be able to make the crossing even if she could be floated off. So I returned to the shelter of the cliffs.

In the early afternoon ... firing now opened from the east and we could see enemy vehicles trundling along the cliff tops east of Veules. They were closing their pincer movement and now there was no way out...

Beach at Veules where Lang was captured

"The end was not long coming. Though determined to fight it out, impossible though the situation was ... Ian and I manned two Lewis guns but it was useless.

The tanks immediately above us opened fire and their third shot blew a great hole in the ship's side; the fourth landed right on the deck. Then I lost consciousness. ...

Highland Division prisoners. Colin Hunter is the person with bandage over eye; on his left (half face) is Derek Lang

"Amongst the ships attempting to take off British and French soldiers was an armed merchant ship called 'Cerons', named after a village south east of Bordeaux. This French ship Cerons approached as close as possible to the beach and soldiers began to board. However, a combination of additional weight and a receding tide on a sandy shoreline caused the ship to become stuck fast and become target practice for the enemy guns. To prevent further casualties the troops made their way back to shore and into captivity. The Cerons sank and even sixty years later a small part of the superstructure is visible at low tide."

Of the 3,200 members of the 51st Highland Division saved from the beaches of Veules les Rose, 110 of them were

The wreck of the Cerons can still be seen at low tide today

rescued by the Newhaven flotillas. But they saved some French also. Twenty-seven year old, Louis Marie Diverres, of Paris, was one of eight wounded Frenchmen – two soldiers and six sailors – who were brought across the Channel in an open motorboat, by Mr Ernie Sayers of Eastbourne.

Sadly, Louis Marie died and was given a military funeral at Langney – the first French soldier in WW2 to be accorded this in England. Two of his French comrades, both injured, were also present at his funeral. The local paper reported that the most touching tribute – a simple bunch of English roses laid on the coffin – was paid to him by the Englishman who had rescued him.

Newspaper article Eastbourne Herald June 22nd 1940

Article Eastbourne Herald, Saturday, 22nd June 1940

FRENCH SOLDIER LAID TO REST AT LANGNEY

Died After Being Brought From His Own Country

In a flower-covered grave at Langney Cemetery lies a young French soldier, who died last Friday after being brought to this country with other comrades. He is the first French combatant ever to be buried in a local cemetery.

The soldier, 27-years-old Louis Marie Diverres, of Paris, was one of the eight wounded Frenchmen –

two soldiers and six sailors – who were rescued from St Valery and brought across the Channel in an open motor boat by a well-known Eastbourne boatman, Mr Ernie ("Glaxo") Sayers.

Diverres was given a military funeral on Wednesday, but amid all the impressive ceremonial the most touching tribute to a gallant poilu was that of the boatman who sat by him in that open boat as it made its hazardous journey from France only a few days before.

It was just a simple bunch of English roses, placed on the coffin by "Glaxo" Sayers and a friend. And to the roses was tied a card which bore the words: "In honour of a very gallant son of France, from two British Allies, Hugh Newham and Ernie Sayers."

Newham had also taken part in the rescue of men from the French coast. …..

….. British soldiers acted as bearers and after the brief committal service three volleys were fired over the grave by the firing party and two buglers sounded the "Last Post" and Reveille, whose echoing notes across the windswept cemetery had a poignancy too deep for words to tell.

In the epilogue of his book, *Churchill's Sacrifice of the Highland Division-France 1940, (Brasseys's 1994; then Endeavour Press Ltd, 2013.)* Saul David summed up the outcome.

"These soldiers of the 51st (Highland) division paid a heavy price for the miscalculations of their government. More than 10,000 were taken prisoner at St Valery, including the members of all three regular Highland battalions. With the 1,000 or so taken on the Somme and in the SAAR, a total of 11,000 soldiers of the Division marched into captivity.

Fatal casualties amongst the Highland infantry alone were over 1,000 with more than four times that number wounded. Balanced against these casualty figures should be the 1,300 rescued from Veules les Roses. ...A total of 3,200 British and 300 French troops were taken off from Veules les Roses on the morning of 12 June. An insignificant number when compared it to the 24,000 General Fortune had hoped to embark, but a small success none the less.

"Hardest hit by the surrender of the Division were the small Highland communities from which the majority of its members were drawn. Many had lost the flower of their manhood at a stroke, some never to return, others not for five years..."

Chapter 4

Liberation

DURING the next four years members of the Highland Division continued to make an overwhelming impact. Most went into captivity but some pulled off spectacular escapes. Neil Campbell and Hugh Oliver of the Camerons got away in the early days of their march to prisoner of war camps in Germany. Surviving for over two weeks they manage to "borrow" a sailing boat from the harbour of St Valery and leave under the noses of the sentries. Campbell, who had been a fisherman in South Uist, navigated his way by the stars until they were picked up by a Navy minesweeper.

Derek Lang was amongst those captured and whose escape and eventual return to Scotland, was one of the most amazing stories. Once in camp at St Pol, many of the battalion would to discuss means of escape with him. Shortly after leaving St Pol, and just two hours into the march to the next camp, he and two friends (Fred and Johnny) made a dash for it, and hid in the hedgerow, remaining there for an hour once the column of prisoners had shuffled past. They were still reasonably near the Channel and they too hoped to find a boat somewhere near Le Touquet and make their escape. But they were recaptured.

Their next escape was from a new prison at Tournai in Belgium where they managed to climb on the wash house roof and observe the movements of the sentries below. For just five minutes their area of the wall was unobserved and at 6:30 on 15th July three of them escaped. Lang made his way down to the south of France; he was then picked up by a Corsican ship and taken to Italy. From there he went to Beirut, then onto the British Consulate in Jerusalem. Yet after these adventures there was no swift return home for he was posted to Cairo and did not see Scotland again until the end of 1942.

The allies landed in Normandy on 4th June 1944; they advanced inland and eventually smashed the German *Seventh Army*. During the Normandy Campaign and throughout the invasion, the Highland Division were serving under the overall command of the Canadian Army. General Field Marshall Bernard Montgomery – showing great sensitivity – wrote to their GOC, General Crerar, saying that all Scotland would be grateful if the Highland Division could liberate St Valery-en-Caux and Veules les Roses.

Once this signal honour was granted, Montgomery deliberately changed the layout of his forces to make it possible. Then on 2nd September, 1944, a four year debt was finally repaid when the re-formed 51st Highland Division – fresh from successes in North Africa, Italy and Normandy – liberated St Valery and learnt from the residents said that all Germans had left two days before.

The leading battalion marching into St Valery that day was headed by Lt Col Derek Lang, who after his amazing experiences was now commanding the 5th Camerons.

"At the end of 1942 I sailed for England via South Africa to take up an appointment at the School of Infantry. I was still there on D-Day but shortly afterwards I received a signal to proceed to France ... within 24 hours I was across the Channel.

I took over the 5th Camerons and shortly afterwards we broke out from Cannes and started the victorious march of liberation through France. As we approached St Valery the whole of the Highland Division were keyed up ... As my leading Company, preceded by five pipers, marched into the town's main square, the local population went wild with delight".

Accompanying Lang during this emotional occasion was Lt Col Bill Bradford, commanding the 5th Black Watch, and together they laid the wreath at the memorial service for the men who had died in 1940.

While many celebrated at St Valery others celebrated at Veules. On the same day that St Valery was freed, the 5th Seaforth were in action. Once they had cut off the Le Havre peninsular, they raced eighty miles eastwards, spotting wrecked vehicles of the old 51st Highland Division lying by the roadside, still with the Stags Head and the Brigade colours visible on their mudguards. They were in Veules les Roses by nightfall.

Alastair Borthwick wrote:

"None of us will ever live such a day again. Though we live to be 90 we will never do it. During their first hours of freedom after four years of German occupation, the French went mad. These people who crowded the village streets walked miles across the fields to line up the roads for us, were happy and excited.., but behind the flag waving and cheering was a profound thankfulness. We were mobbed in every village. Gigantic streamers announced 'Welcome to our Brave Liberators. Others said 'God Save the King' in letters three feet high! There were flags in every window and in ever hand; speeches of welcome were made and cognac offered. We left every village with bouquets piled on the tanks of our motor- bikes."

At 10.30 next day a memorial service was held in the courtyard of the Hotel de France. The Commanding Officer read out a list of 133 officers and men who, on 12th June 1940, had been killed, or died of wounds. The local doctor and the Mayor had tended the wounded. The names seemed to go on forever but eventually, the buglers blew the Last Post and Reveille and the Pipe Major played the Lament.

At 1500 a dance for all ranks was held in the village hall with speeches by the Commanding Officer and the Mayor of Veules and other citizens.

To his regret Lang was not there.

".... I would dearly have liked to walk the four miles along the beach to Veules as I had done before, but time did not permit. Anyway the whole coastline had changed with the massive defences the Germans had built everywhere ... only one thing remained unchanged. On the beach at Veules les Rose, the little British tanker still lay in the sand where we had left her four years early."

Derek Lang did not return to Veules les Roses until he was eighty-six years old.

Chapter 5

COMMEMORATION

IN the years that followed commemorative events took place in all three towns which had been involved in the epic drama that years later is now called *The Other Dunkirk*.

In 1945 the Mayor and Finance & General Purposes Committee of Eastbourne, decided to commemorate Operation Cycle. Two years later on 28th June, and on the beach between the bandstand and the pier at the top of Terminus Road, this was fulfilled, in an event covered by newsreel companies and open to the general public Bronze plaques were attached to every single boat that took part and their full names and their skippers listed in the newspaper.

Article Eastbourne Gazette 28th June 1947
Plaques for Evacuation Boats
Just over seven years since fourteen Eastbourne little fishing and pleasure boats sailed across

The harbour at St Valery

the Channel to St Valery-en-Caux to attempt the evacuation of British troops there, the boat owners are to receive at the hands of the Mayor (Ald. E. C. Martin, J.P.) on behalf of the townspeople, bronze plaques to commemorate their part in the epic of the French Channel ports. …. It is two years now sine the Finance and General Purposes Committee decided to commemorate "Operation Cycle", as the St Valery evacuation attempt was known, by giving these bronze plaques, which will be screwed on to the boats. Since then the plaques have been on order but have been held up through lack of material. But now they been delivered, fourteen of them.

The boatmen concerned will be invited to the beach on Wednesday, and with the Mayor will be the Town Clerk, Mr F.H. Busby, and other officials. The newsreel companies have been invited to film the ceremony and there will be plenty of room for the public to see and hear what is happening.

The boats for which plaques have been made are: Amasis, NN.60, Jessee Huggett, jnr; Golden City, E.83, Messrs Allchorn Bros; Britannia III, NN44, Messrs Sayers Bros; Skylark, NN.71, Allchorn Bros; Olive Joyce JJ.31, Andrew Chester; Lady Doris NN3126, Chas W.G. Bone; My Lassie NN.37, Jessee Huggett, snr; Hibernia NN.47 Michael Hardy; Albion NN.68 Ernest Sayers; Ocean's Gift NN.89, John Prodger, snr; Silver Spray NN.120,William Morgan; Ocean Spray NN.32 Richard Hegarty; Star-n-the-East NN.81 Abraham Matthews; Mispah NN.132, Henry Erridge (deceased).

Then a few years later, a citizen of Veules spotted a bottle of wine bearing the name Cerons on a supermarket shelf, and made an immediate connexion to June 1940. A movement was started with the aim of "liberating" the artillery piece which was mounted on the forecastle of the submerged French vessel. On the cliffs high above the town, that gun now stands proud between the British and Scottish flags. Nearby is a superb memorial erected in 2015 and dedicated

The clifftop above Veules les Roses, with gun from the wreck of the Cerons and commemorative plaques

to the memory of the brave soldiers who gave their lives in the service of France and Britain.

The Mayor of Veules contacted the Mayor of Cerons and after the usual formalities an official twinning was enacted between the two villages.

Finally, in June 2000, General Sir Derek Lang, now the eighty-six-year-old, led a proud group of his veterans in commemoration of the 60th anniversary. There were many moving moments as wreaths were laid at monuments and services were conducted at the immaculately tended graveyards which hold so many young men of the 51st – some known only to God.

Chapter 6

REMEMBRANCE

ONCE twinning had been established between Alfriston and Veules les Roses many things – from deep friendships, mutual visits and joint research – developed rapidly and we soon realised that close connections between the Cuckmere Valley and Normandy had been in place for generations.

In 1042 Edith married Edward the Confessor – the King of England. By 1045, she was the owner of 'Ferles' – now Frog Firle – the extensive lands below Hindover to the south west of Alfriston. After 1066, William the Conqueror placed most local land into the hands of his half-brother, Robert, Count of Mortain.

By 1086 he had endowed the Abbey of St Mary of Grestain in Normandy with estates near Alfriston – the Priories of Michelham and Wilmington as well as Ferles. All were controlled from Normandy and full details are in the Domesday Book.

Thus what happened nine days after Dunkirk and three months after D-Day was just another link in a lengthy historical chain. So as we revelled in our long-standing mutual history, we decided both to rejoice and commemorate together. During the first weekend of September 2014, we would celebrate the liberation of Veules; nine months later, on 13th June 2015, we would commemorate the 75th anniversary of the attempted evacuation. We hoped that representatives from the successors of the Highland Regiments of the 51st Highland Division could be persuaded to join us on both occasions: the task of arranging this fell on me.

So I wrote to the Commanding Officer of the 51st Highland, 7th Battalion, Royal Regiment of Scotland, whose headquarters are in Perth. I explained the background; how the 4th Seaforths, 5th Gordons and 1st Black Watch had been closely involved; how our two towns were now twinned and what we hoped to do in the way of simple poignant memorial.

"We, and the Mayor of Veules les Roses, would like to issue an invitation for some pipers from the regiment to be present during the celebratory weekend. Everyone would consider it a great honour if they could come and would give them the warmest of welcomes"

Lieutenant Colonel Col Peter Little, the Commanding Officer, telephoned me the moment he received my letter.

He was so pleased that the history was finally being made available to a wider public. He would send 50 soldiers – pipers and men – to join us. Some were presently stationed in Scotland, others in Germany. The contingent would be led by his Adjutant, Captain Charlie Grant, whose father, Brigadier Charles Grant, had commanded the 51st Highland Brigade, the modern successors to the Division.

The group from Germany had a relatively easy journey. The group from Perth drove hundreds of miles to Newhaven and took the overnight ferry to Dieppe – sleeping in their transport when they could.

That weekend in September 2014, will long be remembered. The formal events began at 10 am on the Saturday when Captain Charles Grant assembled his contingent near the seafront. With drummers and pipers

Soldiers marching through the town

Commemorative Service in L'eglise Saint-Martin

they marched through the town to L'eglise Saint-Martin for a memorial service, at the end of which the Piper played the last lament

Then in a small square, now named Place des Ecossais a Veules, a plaque was unveiled in honour of the Scottish Division who contributed towards the liberation all those years ago.

Afterwards, led by Captain Grant, everyone walked up to the special area in the cemetery dedicated to those who died in the final hours, nine days after Dunkirk.

By each grave, someone – whether from Veules or Alfriston – stood with a red rose in their hand. But the largest group were the young soldiers of the present Royal

A la Mémoire des Soldats, Sous-Officiers,
Officiers de la 51st Highland Division
(51ème Division Ecossaise) qui,
les 10-11-12 Juin 1940, se sont battus et sont tombés
sur notre sol pour que vive notre liberté !
Revenus en libérateurs le 2 Septembre 1944.
Ils sont vivants dans notre Coeur !

To the Memory of the Soldiers,
Non-Commissioned Officers and Officers
of the 51st Highland Division who,
on June the 10th-11th-12th, 1940, fought and fell
on our soil that we might live in Freedom.
On September the 2nd, 1944
they returned as Liberators.
They are forever in our hearts.

Captain Charles Grant and Jean Claude Claire (Maire) unveiling commemorative plaque

Pipers marching to cemetery

Regiment. In turn they placed the flower on the grave, stepped back, spoke the name aloud and saluted. But many only said 'Unknown Soldier.'

As one young soldier placed the rose on the ground he realised that the person at rest

Highlanders in dedicated area in cemetery

Soldier with rose at headstone

Artefacts recovered from beach in dedicated museum at Veules

was just 19 years old. That was his age, and as he saluted there were tears in his eyes.

There were tears in mine too as I recited lines from the famous poem that in the United Kingdom is always spoken at commemorative services for the fallen

"They shall not grow old as we that are left grow old
Age shall not weary them nor the years condemn
At the going down of the sun and in the morning
We will remember them"

Next there was the inauguration of the exhibition – in Clos Saint Vincent – of military artefacts that over the years had been discovered in the shifting sands of the coastline.

June Goodfield and Jean Claude Claire receiving coat-of-arms

The hospitality was magnificent: a buffet lunch; a wonderful dinner; dancing and music by Les Crustaceans, the famous musicians of Veules. Captain Grant presented Jean Claude Claire and June Goodfield with the coat-of-arms of the Royal Regiment. When in a moment of frivolity JG asked whether she might be adopted as the mascot, the answer was a resounding 'no'. When asked why, Charlie Grant said 'because you are not a goat!'

The soldiers also found time to time to walk the battlefield and study details of the campaign – which the newly joined members of the brigade would write up when they returned to Scotland. Finally, they piled back into their vehicles and began the long journey across the Channel and up to Perth.

Captain Charlie Grant wrote to me the very day they arrived back.

"It is hard to stress just how enjoyable the weekend in Veules les Roses was for me personally ... and for every member of the Royal Regiment who took part. ... Being a keen military historian, I was fascinated by the history and walking the battlefield really brought it to life.

I felt that the service, the plaque unveiling and the ceremony in the cemetery were all very moving ... but I have to confess that it was the overwhelming degree of hospitality that blew me away. ... I genuinely meant it when I said to the assembled group that I cannot think of any other occasion when I have been made to feel as welcomed as we were made to feel by the people of Veules les Roses."

The Commanding Officer also wrote to us all:

"Dr June, Deputy Lord Lieutenant, Monsieur Le Maire, and Honoured Guests of the Twinning Associations from both sides of the Channel. I send these words as Commanding Officer of 51st Highland, 7th Battalion, The Royal Regiment of Scotland, now the sole Reserve Infantry Battalion in the Highlands. ...

... thank you so much for looking after my lads so well: to a man, they all commented on how generous the people of Veules were and how wonderfully they were hosted. I hope that my fortunes will change next summer and that I can take up the kind invitation to join you in France, when you will mark the 75thAnniversary of the terrible fighting and evacuation. For now, may I say thank you for everything you have done over the years to save Highland soldiers' lives, and for what you have done since in remembering the losses and honouring both our Veterans and servicemen in all branches of the Armed Forces. We are privileged and proud to include you all as our friends."

The following year, on Saturday 13th June 2015, we were all again in Veules for a day of moving ceremonies, both commemorating the 75th anniversary of the final evacuation from France and remembering those who were killed. This was an even bigger occasion: over 4,000 people attended – from the British Embassy in Paris, the Elysees Palace, the Prefet from Dieppe; many people from Alfriston, such as Charles Anson, the Deputy Lord Lieutenant of East Sussex, who for some time had been Press Secretary to Her Majesty The Queen.

Preceded by the Pipe and Drums of the 51st Highland, 7th Battalion, The Royal Regiment of Scotland – all magnificent in full ceremonial Highland dress- together we marched up to the simple cemetery at the top of the hill,. The soldiers were led by the battalion Commanding Officer, Lt Col Piers Strudwick, along with the former Queen Mother's Piper and senior officers of the French Army and Navy.

Opposite each headstone stood one soldier and one local child. Each soldier announced the name of their dead forebear and laid a red rose on his grave, then the young local boy or girl – local child laid a poppy they had made at school.

The day started grey and overcast, but as the Last Post sounded the clouds broke up and cleared away to a fine sunny morning. The ceremony ended with the moving hymn *Amazing Grace* played by the Scottish Pipe Band.

Afterwards everyone moved to the ceremony on the cliff top up the path along which Captain Derek Boileau Lang

Dedicating the cliff path named after Captain Derek Lang

and his colleagues were marched after they were captured. The footpath was now named "Sentier Derek Lang" in honour of that eminent Scottish soldier. His daughter, Sarah, was present, so too was his grandson with his wife and two great-grandchildren.

The sunny afternoon culminated with a wonderful dedication ceremony by the gun and where a new memorial to the fallen of both nations was revealed. The people at Veules les Roses had worked hard to construct this – a huge stone monument listing the names of the fallen. After this was unveiled various representatives walked forward in turn to lay roses and make a short speech.

The schoolchildren of Veules were with us again: some carried a white balloon with the name of a soldier killed in

Newly erected monument to those who fell

Walking forward to lay roses

the final days – or just bearing the words 'unknown soldier'. Together they sang and then released the balloons that floated high into a brilliantly sunny sky towards the east.

Balloons heading east

The gala dinner that evening was superb and one highlight was Charles Anson's second speech. He lives in Alfriston and is a great supporter of the Twinning activities. Given that the Queen and Prince Philip were in Normandy in 2014 for the 70th anniversary of D-Day, Charles had sent full details to Buckingham Palace, with accompanying photographs, of what we had researched. These documents are now in the archives of Buckingham Palace too. Charles had brought a warm letter from Her Majesty that was read out several times during the weekend.

Charles Anson relaying a message from Her Majesty the Queen

"I am happy to report to M.Le Maire, Jean Claude Claire, and all our friends here, that I informed Buckingham Palace of these commemorations and that Her Majesty wishes them well. On 13 May 2015, I received a letter from the Palace confirming that Her Majesty had received the brief outline and photographs illustrating the current relationship between Alfriston and Veules les Roses, and sends her good wishes."

EPILOGUE

A week or so later more fascinating information appeared.

First, M.le Maire contacted me. Four days after the balloon launch he received a letter from someone living on the East German border. A balloon had come down in her garden bearing the name of the soldier and the contact details in Veules. She was very moved and asked them to please tell her how this occurred.

Then one year later a small square in Veules les Roses was named in honour of Tom Renouf, a distinguished soldier in the Black Watch and General Lang's right hand man in supporting the veterans.

A few weeks before this, I had been in the Newhaven home of a seamstress, Jan Stevens, who was altering one of my skirts. We talked a little about the days after Dunkirk and she revealed that she had worked at Moss Brothers, Market Street, Lewes, for many years. This was not the famous Moss Bros that hires out garments for exotic occasions, but a family firm who made clothes – mostly Scottish kilts from tartan sent down from the north. Jan worked on piece rates: sewing up 60 kilts a day from cloth that had been steamed for 48 hours. So the pleats were in place before the seamstress got to work.

The finished garments were sent up to Scotland and it is highly likely that some of the 51st Highland Regiment who went over to Normandy in WW2, were wearing kilts made in East Sussex. Jan skills were such that clearly the 7 yards tartan would continue to provide adequate protection … from everything!

We all – French, Scots, English – see each other regularly. As Charles Anson said, "When we started our twinning relationship we could never have imagined what we would discover and achieve together. Our memories of 75 years ago may be poignant and sad, yet they are also a testament to friendship, humanity and the strength of the human spirit. We, in Alfriston, take great pride in this association and look forward to the next … well, let me say … 100 years at least!"

ACKNOWLEDGEMENTS

THIS book depends on many peoples' personal recollections and valuable memories or written histories, extracts of which are widely used in the text.

The author owes a great debt to many people and wishes to thank:

Her Majesty, The Queen for interest and letter of good wishes

Dame Vera Lynn

The Highland Regiments in Perth

M. le Maire, Jean Claude Claire, Chevalier Order Legion d'Honneur

Jean Louis Angelini

Francoise Marinier

Mr Daniel Ducau

Babette Kundrat

Marilyn Eva

Lt Colonel Peter Little

Major C M Grant

Brigadier (Ret'd) C S Grant OBE

Sarah Hunt and family

The late Tom Renouf

Kathleen Renouf

George Renouf

Helen Kidd

Charles Anson

Mark Hurst

Tony Palmer

Jim Taylor

Museum of Newhaven

Museum Clos Saint Vincent, Veules les Roses

Eastbourne press

Allchorn family

Ian Shearer

Cheryl Lutring

Ryan Gearing

Supported by

51st Highland Division (web: https://51hd.co.uk)

The Ross Bequest Trust

The Write House

BIBLIOGRAPHY

Books & Articles

Delaforce, Patrick, *Monty's Marauders, 51st Highland Division in the Second World War*, Tom Donovan Publishing Ltd, 1977

Garside, Tom Wardle, *Escaping St Valery June 1940* (account provided by his son Jim)   http://.51hd.co.uk/accounts/tom_garside_st_valery

Innes, Bill: *The Impossible Odds*, Birlinn Ltd, 2012

Lang, Derek, *Return to St Valery*, Leo Cooper Ltd, 1974

Renouf, Tom, *Black Watch: Liberating Europe & Catching Himmler – My Extraordinary WW2 with the Highland Division*,

Little, Brown Book Group, 2011

Saul, David, *Churchill's Sacrifice of the Highland Division – France 1940*,

Brasseys 1994 and Endeavour Press 2013

Quest for a Lost Father, BBC/co.uk/print history/ ww2peopleswar: labris@btinternet.com .

10th-12th June 1940, *The Fierce Battle*, published by Association Pays de Caux Terre d'Histoire, France

Museums and Websites

Four Scottish Military Museums record the history of the Division: The Black Watch in Perth; the Highlanders Museum at Fort George; the Gordon Highlanders Museum in Aberdeen; the Argyll & Sutherland Highlanders Museum in Stirling.

However, the best way to contact regimental museums, is the Army Museums Ogilby Trust Website that provides links to all the individual Army museums. https://www.armymuseums.org.uk

The 51st Highland Division Web Site is https://51hd.co.uk/